THE ORIGIN OF BUTTERFLIES

ROMEO ORIOGUN

Published by Akashic Books
©2018 Romeo Oriogun

ISBN: 978-1-61775-638-2

Printed in China through Four Colour Print Group, Louisville, Kentucky
First printing

Akashic Books
Brooklyn, New York, USA
Ballydehob, Co. Cork, Ireland
Twitter: @AkashicBooks
Facebook: AkashicBooks
E-mail: info@akashicbooks.com
Website: www.akashicbooks.com

African Poetry Book Fund
Prairie Schooner
University of Nebraska
110 Andrews Hall
Lincoln, Nebraska 68588

TABLE OF CONTENTS

Preface by Jericho Brown 4

Loneliness 7
Departure 8
Kumbaya 10
Saddest Night Alive 12
Gay Boy History 14
Elegy for a Burnt Friend 16
Coming Out 17
How to Survive the Fire 19
Denial 20
The Origin of Butterflies 21
Boomerang 23
Boy, 24
At the Police Checking Point 26
Orlando 27
Pink Club 28
Exile 30
To the Boy who Flew Away 32
Resurrection 34

Acknowledgments 36

PREFACE
by Jericho Brown

The poems of Romeo Oriogun's *The Origin of Butterflies* mean to take loneliness and turn it into a psychedelic adventure. The collection begins, "I do not want to write how lonely / a car parked under the rain / in a deserted road sings." Yet before the opening poem ends, we feel anything but parked. The surreal and even absurd ride includes, "birds die & are reborn as clouds" and "my body / is full of strange men begging to live."

This is a beginning. And why? Why does Oriogun insist that we move forward with him through an impossible language he headlong creates in the midst of drafting each line? Because supposedly foreign experiences require a combination of words that allow us to see the human heart beating in the midst of what we are trained to condemn. Oriogun himself cannot even hear the music his own body makes unless it is first approved by some outsider: "… my neighbor presses her ear against the wall / to hear the voice of heaven / falling from a mouth made beautiful by sin." What world is this where the sounds of one's own voice gets called "sin," where one's loneliness is only magnified by his neighbor's clandestine curiosity?

Well, while Oriogun is a poet of the surreal, he is also a poet of direct statement. He may tilt our view with mystery, but he never leaves us confused. Here are the first few lines of the unapologetic "Gay Boy History":

> What they want is for me to say I'm sorry
> but I'm beautiful like a museum.
> That means I'm full of history,
> that means I was here before the white men
> came with God.
>
> What if I tell you I was once broke & hidden
> and starving & had to eat my shadow

to survive?
Ask me about migration,
why I intend to shake my tail feathers
before a man in order to have
my passport stamped.
People like me have been hiding in deserts,
willing the night to hide our songs in winds.
Besides, everyone needs freedom . . .

The Origin of Butterflies is a book of disagreements with one's own homeland. The speaker throughout is self-assured in spite of his feeling of exile to the desert of himself in his own country. He is unabashedly black and brazenly physical.

Yet there is compassion here, a need beyond necessary rebellion for acknowledgment, community, and friendship in lines like: "People like me have been hiding" and "Besides, everyone needs freedom." In all of this book's *Whitmanesque,* "I celebrate myself and sing myself" attitude, Oriogun also finds himself bereft in the face of real-life political danger and the fact that a life of freedom can lead to violent retribution for him and his friends. This is the case in many poems, including, "Elegy for a Burnt Friend" ("Forgive me, I drank old wine / as a mob marked your body"), and "How to Survive the Fire" ("I tell you the truth, my mouth is clean / but on my tongue are cities / where boys are beaten to death").

In all, Romeo Oriogun is a poet of the austere lyric that, through its yielding toward sensuality, begins to sound like history itself:

Come into dark, let me sing
the night through your body
like a man learning how to worship God
in a strange land.
("Coming Out")

But the grand gestures of love and romance reach forward in time. This voice knows how love begins, just as much as it knows of Facebook and twenty-first-century massacres of queer people as far away or as close as Orlando, Florida. These two impulses have everything to do with the expansive and contemporary nature of Oriogun's own reading. (He goes as far as directly referencing other international poets, including Safia Elhillo and Danez Smith.)

Yes, I take some pride in watching the development of black gay poets all over the world. Somehow, our existence as people capable of something other than sex is still questionable. I know how important it is for a poet like Oriogun to exist . . . to fight . . . to flail around with words until he finds a language—however exacting and wild—for this life we continue to characterize and defend as human. I also know he's just the man for the job, or as he would say in the title poem, "Give a man words & he will build a castle / full of darkness & light."

LONELINESS

I do not want to write how lonely
a car parked under the rain
in a deserted road sings,
but I've been on this journey for ten years,
searching for a boy to translate the sweetness in my language;
searching for a door out of the fear sitting inside my throat.
Nothing is constant; birds die & are reborn as clouds,
leaves go into the earth to become songs,
yet my love is passed down as sin,
nailed to the wall in a city where my body
is full of strange men begging to live,
nailed to balls of fire falling from the mouths
of preachers shouting in fields.
At night I sit in silence to hear my body
mingle with the stars in darkness.
I know how loneliness sits in a deserted town
and plays dead songs from parched lips.
I know how a body enters itself
to hide desire behind sadness.
I've been sitting for a long time,
waiting for a boy to heal the confusion
falling in my heart.
The rain keeps falling & I don't know
if the birds rising in my heart
is my body saying it's alright to love
this wildness walking into a city on fire.

DEPARTURE

i was born with a graveyard
—Safia Elhillo

i do know about the hate that sinks a name
& turns water into homes eating boys,
& i cannot speak because my mouth is a grave.
My father's ghost ate a boy found in the hands of another boy
& his bones look like the sun dying on my skin,
& every day men hurting bodies filled with love
are praised as heroes,
hailed as saviors opening bodies
into fields eaten by locusts.

i was born to be darkness hiding under a cave
& i know the weight of exile in a body;
the origin of bodies looking into faces
with gratitude, leaving a part of them
in bistros to forget how they prayed
to the winds to ferry them over waves.

the maestro said all art is full of departure.
i was born to hold a boy in a bus station,
shake him loose like a house leaking memories
& tell him go, run, bleed
into a language that knows the meaning of freedom.

tired of running, of biting into oranges,
i open my body into pain & bring out your words:
faggot, sin, bones waiting for the tongue of fire,
& i let them slice me, burn me.

i was born into a war. My God's duty is to hide
the honey dripping from my mouth,
& i write the names of lovers leaving into a kingdom of sand.
i let it grow on their tongues so they won't forget
how they lived in the dark before finding Agadez's
pathway, a road across the sea.

i worship the day because it survived the night,
& i'm in a bus station
saying bye to boys searching for cities
where they can hold hands & walk on beaches.
& i know what it means to live here
with words invented for hate, with wounds asked to be silent.
& when they leave i want to whisper into ears
filled with dunes of the desert,
do not forget i still live here.

KUMBAYA

I cannot make this up.
   Sunlight sneaks behind dark curtains

     & you sit up, say the light is here again.

The streets hum with voices,
    vehicles run into the rising sun,
      my neighbor presses her ear against the wall
        to hear the voice of heaven
          falling from a mouth made beautiful by sin.

    I want to find home in the rooms of your veins,
allow you to carry me as you flee into the day,

    as you look back to stop your shadows from holding my hands.

In your room, your father smashes our bones against the wall,

 our blood mingles, sings kumbaya as it streaks into the rug.

Tell me this is not love,
   tell me this is not how couples run into sunsets.

   Tell me this is not the universe saying love is eternal
to two bodies traveling through the sea as salt;
   two bodies sitting on sands
in a map that doesn't die.

He digs me out of your stomach.

He says, *No son of mine is going to be a faggot.*

   I allow light to preserve me; I allow it to slash me into songs
traveling through the forest softly as dew.

Here's my body, take it.

   Here's my song searching for space within your lips,

open, sing it.

When they came for me with knives & sticks,

I became songs falling through rain.

Do not be afraid, I will always be here.

Just step into the wet sky,
open your mouth, sing,

   sing baby.

SADDEST NIGHT ALIVE

It always starts with your silence, your body running away,
even though you are here & the music is still playing
and all I want is to dance, just to dance, baby,
but you are really not here & the sea is always hungry
and everyone is watching how you will feed it.
We are in a movie, we are acting,
but you keep saying this is not right.
I want to know who made love so wrong.
The director is screaming, his veins are bulging,
I'm shouting leave him alone, they were the words I shouted
when they lynched you in my dreams.
Can't you see my buttons are undone & waiting for your fingers?
Can't you see the leaves are falling?
It's the season for wearing new skin,
for pretending you don't love the boy who rode across your mouth
last night, & I understand you are afraid
because your friend's father gave him up to the police
on his birthday, & I know it's a shitty way to celebrate a new year,
but I do not want to beg for love,
I do not want to steal into your dreams.
The DJ is playing my favorite song,
bodies are moving like fireflies dancing by the riverside.
You are leaving. In my hand is a glass of gin & tonic.
I'm learning how to live with this fear of not finding love
in this city, how to watch my waves run back into the sea
like a dog cursed with the luck of finding dead lovers.
The director is shouting but you are already gone
and I'm leaving, drunk & in tears.
The music is still playing, still calling our hearts like clouds

waiting for the miracle of wings.
They will write this as the saddest night alive,
but it won't mean a thing to us, we've been hurting
before the earth put to birth.

GAY BOY HISTORY

What they want is for me to say I'm sorry
but I'm beautiful like a museum.
That means I'm full of history,
that means I was here before the white men
came with God.

What if I tell you I was once broke & hidden
and starving & had to eat my shadow
to survive?
Ask me about migration,
why I intend to shake my tail feathers
before a man in order to have
my passport stamped.
People like me have been hiding in deserts,
willing the night to hide our songs in winds.
Besides, everyone needs freedom,
maybe I will stay if I can fill my throat
with wine & allow a man to suck it
under the moon, but I'm not stupid
and my body is not ripe for burning.

Do you really know why I want to walk
my body into a gay bar
and make my mouth dance into freedom?
I'm illegal & wild.
I'm forbidden
like an apple waiting to be plucked.
I'm empty
and my body is crying to be filled.

Do not ask me about the hunger
turning me into a wolf;
do not ask me about the name
I keep whispering.
Before the night is dead,
I intend to tear your body into questions
and leave you with fire running through your hair.

ELEGY FOR A BURNT FRIEND

Because the night is silent,
the trees will search for a voice,
the wind will fill a body with sorrowful songs.
Forgive me, I drank old wine
as a mob marked your body.
There is nowhere to say enough,
nowhere to breathe in the open sea
without salt stinging your throat;
nowhere to wash our body in water & become free.
There was mockery on the spot
where your hand touched the blood on your shirt.
The voice said, *You are fallen ashes, a mirror*
of something unnatural, the dark side of God.
This was the point my mouth should have poured water
over your burning skin.
Forgive me, there was a pipe lying so close to another man;
there was a fire burning nearby & I ran into a dark street,
where I called your name in silence & said *live,*
knowing people like us will always be hunted.
I remember the night you licked the salt
in my palm & said do not be afraid to live in your skin.
Maybe you knew, you knew one day your screams
would stretch my throat & my silence would break
out of a darkness hard as a wall.
I'm trying hard not to cry,
I'm saying the earth ate the moon last night
but someone will mock your last prayers
and my skin will burst into a river.

COMING OUT

The woman on the bar stool knows your body
is a journey into songs,
the door into a moth flirting with fire,
which means there's a pretty boy
living under your skin.
I do not wish to come to you
but I can't help it & you look drunk, like a man
seeking a way out of himself
or a way into the beginning of his voice.
The city knows how to kill a man like you
and on the face of some men
I can see you burning.
Tonight you take your first step into music,
saying your body knows how to beat a path
through hell & back,
saying angels do not die in song
you are daring like a throat accepting the fire of tequila.
Across you in a dark booth, I want to scream
silently: "Do not dance,
do not give in to the wild beat flowing through your heart!"
But you are dancing like a boy drowning inside
his blood & all my body
can do is pray your soul into a bird's wings
and hope the wind calls you home.
Do you know the first thing about fire?
Have you seen a mouth calling God
only to find a body rising in smoke?
The city does not want
to hear your song flowing through a bird,

they don't want you dancing inside a rainbow.
Come into the dark before a man
greets your body with violence.
Come into dark, let me sing
the night through your body
like a man learning how to worship God
in a strange land.

HOW TO SURVIVE THE FIRE

The first rule of survival is to run.
I tell you this so you understand how memories
are floods drowning a lonely man,
how the sight of a man burning
in a park stays with you;
his voice becoming yours at night.
There's no boy hiding in my throat.
I tell you the truth, my mouth is clean
but on my tongue are cities
where boys are beaten to death.
Say Lagos, say Onitsha, say Lafia,
say cities where the only freedom
for a man who loves another man is to leave.
I tell you this so you understand my silence,
understand why I crawled into my voice;
I do not want to die.
There is nowhere safe in this city of mine
and songs of freedom are just what they are.
You have to see nails drawing blood
from a swollen head
before you understand why God turned
his face from Christ & whispered, *Run.*

DENIAL

In the dark, my lover with a halo
offered his skin to me & said *eat*.
At night everything becomes a dream;
becomes real; becomes a dish.
The skin of a lover is a fish baked with olives.
In my mouth he multiplies
into flavors that make love to the tongue.
When I was little my playmates
washed their fears into my soul & giggled.
There was no shame lying under my shirt
as I carried them into the eye of the sun.
I know tomorrow you will hide from me
as I walk across your shadow.
Do not try to explain, I know there's always a beach
waiting for the souls of slain lovers,
but no one walks into death willingly.
It is a fact that everyone has eaten a part of God
before tasting the fall of man.
When the sun is high there are a thousand men waiting
to mock my loneliness with pictures of death.
Tell me, what passes your lips as a mob
lynches my body into a wounded song?
I want to remember you
as my body falls out of your mouth,
but my song reminds me of how you betrayed me
thrice in a room filled with angry men.
There's a part of me willing to forgive
but unlike Christ I can't find my voice.

THE ORIGIN OF BUTTERFLIES

Give a man a piano
and his fingers will find music,
but when grief lives in walls
what music will a mouth produce?
My hands are beginning to find space
deep in my room.
Say a butterfly once lived in your throat,
that's to say you once held the winds
under your skin;
that's to say you once rode bicycles
on dusty roads;
that's to say you once saw pregnant women
and thought of flowers hiding behind laughter.
On the blank page of your life,
what will be the next sentence?
Write death, sadness, a little boy
singing about silence in a room
made dark by his mother's shadow.
Last night I saw a butterfly break
darkness with the colors of her wings.
She rose gently to the moon with songs
within her body.
Give a man words & he will build a castle
full of darkness & light.
There is a place where butterflies live.
Mother said happiness can come from sadness.
On the next page of my life
I wrote only one word: *Happiness.*
I watched it grow from my book

and break the night into fragments of stars.
Someone once said, *When the sun is dead*
we take light in small sips.
I do not know what it means,
I only saw stars falling as butterflies.

BOOMERANG

Before lynching me into sad songs,
walk me into your father's body,
watch as I fold a boy into his heart.
Do not be afraid, I will lead him into love
and show him where the fear comes from.
There are boots always running inside my head,
that's why my body tastes like small wars.
A battered soldier walks on my skin,
bringing trauma to every boy I will love.
This is the beginning of something deeper than fear,
of boys walking with kites hidden under their clothes.
Save your tears, I'm saving your best shot for last.
I will walk him through every burning boy,
through every skin receiving your gift of nails.
I wish I could end this but I don't know how;
I don't know how to make you see
the birds dying in my heart.
I can only touch your fingers curled around a trigger
and pray you see how each squeeze is a bullet
killing a song inside boys filled with love.

BOY,

born black & gay / born light & flowers / thought
the word / for house was rainbow /

a place full of songs / for a boy filled with sweet water /
whose mother walked / from the old town /

dressed in dreams / & sermons /
about hell & gay angels on fire /

he knew the price for skin / he swayed / between
earth & fire / between salt & blood /

every boy he knew stayed outside / his mouth / only I /
knew his story / boy locked at home /

waiting for his mother & the girl / the girl of milk & /
brown teeth / filled with the moon /

skin naked like creation / every time he tried / he
got burnt / every time he tried / her skin poured back /

into her hands / only I / knew the silence of their eyes /
creatures hungry / for what hands / cannot provide /

find language strange / under heat / under skin / drowning /
with expectations / language moving opposite two lips /

waiting for something / to tear them apart / grateful for
my voice / saying litany for the lost /

you can never / force home into a body / already home /
you can never / break songs / of sunrise / into dark spirits /

only I / knew how his mother / begged their tongues /
into a ritual of secrets /

when we play at night / I still see him / son of water & love /
telling his body / about flowers dancing under water

AT THE POLICE CHECKING POINT

He chewed his kola nut softly,
as his finger rested on the trigger.

I had to stop the boy under me
from crying.

He said: *I heard some ass fuckers
are traveling this way.*

We held our mouths
with burnt bones,
gave him fifty naira
as a passing fee,
and went our way.

The girl who sat
with her lover
wet her trousers.

There was a boy,
whose name I can't remember,
all he kept saying was:
Drive to the border.

ORLANDO

There's no song alive tonight. Even in cities
where a man in love with another man is a bird
with a wounded chest, your cry was heard.
Before free men became home for bullets
and a throat collapsed on a dance beat,
we held hands on an empty street,
two boys hiding in the dark,
talking about exile as a gateway to freedom.
We whispered Orlando, as the city gave birth
to two women dancing to an erotic song
in a moon hanging below a palm tree.
No one knew hatred would sprout
along the spine of a man,
allowing gunshots to silence
the voice of lovers.
No one knew about knives
boring holes in the night sky.
The radio said the lucky ones are dead,
the unlucky will wake up at night
to live in a bullet piercing sleep.
We who are endangered will keep
searching for a place to call home.

PINK CLUB

In the club at Garki we dance in silence
because we are illegal; because the man
who tastes of gin also tastes of fear;
because the club is hidden in the eye of the night,
in a place where man dancing into another man
is a beautiful song humming deep within my veins.
& I want to know heaven in the mouth of a boy,
& we are crying because we are free;
because there's no sin inside dance;
because your father's voice is a far country
where sadness resides, call it home,
call it a place where boys who taste of flowers
are stolen at night.
You know sanctuary is where your hips
grow feathers & fly.
The drag queen dancing close to you
tastes of whisky & you want to lie inside her,
close your eyes & walk away into her voice;
you want to fill your bones with wine
till a boy swims into your hands.
The bar sings of freedom & we keep wrecking it
because for once you are a butterfly
fluttering on the tongue of a boy
who called you beautiful,
& I'm lying on a sofa because I'm dreaming
of cities filled with freedom,
because I'm free to breathe in the wet skin
of lovers swaying to a song
that is the road to a city of light;

free to drink pink gin from a pink bar.
& Abuja sleeps because I'm free to raise
a city where boys who love other boys
are free to hold hands in the throat
of the boy dancing beside me,
& you are laughing because this is strange,
because the first time you heard about this club
you thought about the boy who met love on Facebook,
who walked through his fear to meet a lynching
in a dark street, who couldn't report to the police
because a gay man is a fire waiting to happen.
Neon lights run along our limbs as we lose ourselves
to dance,
& the day is on my tongue & I'm tipsy,
& all I want to do is sit before the sun
& drink rainwater on the skin of the boy
who called my mouth a city of refuge.

EXILE

Tell me again about the sugar lying on your skin;
about the dream where God stole you from your bed;
about the boy who wrote *faggot* under your name;
about your mama writing *dead* on your favorite picture;
about your street rising up in a wave to pound you into dust.

Tell me about the fear you hide under your oversized T-shirt.
You do not talk, even when we sit in darkness
on the pier & watch as fishermen pull out grief
in the bodies of fishes. Under moonlight your skin
cracks into the finest black & I want to tell you
how sadness makes us lost & visible.

You remain silent even when comets
drop into water & I know you are thinking about
being outed on Twitter; about your house
buzzing with the word *forbidden*;
about the holy water waiting to chase
out the spirits singing under your skin.
You want to drink out of my happiness
and I'm happy to share, but there's
also this fear I hide in music,
and when the radio plays a song filled with darkness
I want to lie in its mouth & get lost.

The tide is going out
and your head on my shoulder
is a boat getting ready to walk on water,
and I know you must leave,

because home has become a place
that eats the bones of young boys.

TO THE BOY WHO FLEW AWAY

You know the taste of jam;
the taste of blood breathing after a beating;
the taste of your mama's song as prayers
waiting to change you.
& every day I see the fear breaking your body
into horizons too far to be reached.
Your letter sits on my table,
telling me about your departure,
because lightning doesn't strike twice
& your body still breathes with bruises.
How did we come to this;
to be water begging for skin,
to be songs begging for love?
I want to know a boy
whose name is the door out of darkness.
& I'm dancing alone in the dark
because sometimes your body is your lover
and it demands to be worshipped.
What did they say when they flew you
across cities?
I kneel down to touch the back of God,
to ask for angels falling at dusk
into the hands of a lonely boy.
What is a prayer if not a wish?
If not a boy waiting for me with rivers
coming home under his palms;
if not you wondering why all the boys you met
in my city are broken into dried bamboo
afraid of burning,

as the sun bathes in the mouth of the living
while we wait for whatever body salvation walks in.
Is it true that you walked into a party
with a white lover & heard the world breathe out?
There are prayers too heavy to fly to heaven.
I want to love a boy
who tastes of fear & still smiles.

RESURRECTION

after Danez Smith

I sing this body back to life,
name the black keys of a piano
after boys finding air again
& watch as they rise into music;
as they eat wings of chicken
& find home in bottles of wine
while their bodies sing hosanna.
This is not a dream,
we are reclaiming lost souls
into new bodies;
we are walking past jails
with our mouths full of love;
we are hugging boys confused
about the light humming in their bones;
we are saying go home,
go meet your mama because you are
the prayer she's been waiting for.
& no man is waiting with nails beaten into sticks,
& no man is saying show me how you are hell,
& there's no crowd wishing you were not born.
Everywhere, ashes are reclaiming bones & names
& skin & bodies.
Bruises & scars are growing into lullabies
& there's no moth dancing by the fire,
no boy running into the night.
We have stitched the ocean into a continent
where black boys can walk in gardens
without their hearts falling out,

& lovers can trap the sun between wet skin
as they fold the earth into mouths
& breathe out seeds.

ACKNOWLEDGMENTS

"Departure," "Kumbaya," and "Saddest Night Alive" were first
published in *Brittle Paper*.

"Boy," was first published in *Praxis*.